Kochstraße

Schmidt-Buch-Verlag Wernigerode

Impressionen aus der bunten Stadt
Impressions of the colourful town

Es fotografierte Thorsten Schmidt

WERNIGERODE

Den Text schrieb Uwe Lagatz

Vom Turm der Liebfrauenkirche eröffnet sich eine weite Aussicht über die Dächer der bunten Stadt bis hoch hinauf zum Brocken.

From the tower of the Church of Our Lady (Liebfrauenkirche) – there is a sweeping panoramic vista above the rooftops of the colourful town as far as the Brocken.

Wernigerode eint Tradition und Moderne. Seit 150 Jahren gleichermaßen beliebtes Urlaubsziel und leistungsfähiger Wirtschaftsstandort verfügt die Stadt über zahlreiche touristische Anziehungspunkte ebenso wie über eine innovative Infrastruktur. So überqueren am "Altstadtkreisel" seit 2006 die Züge der Harzer Schmalspurbahnen mit Volldampf den neuzeitlichen Autoverkehr. Den Weg zum nahe gelegenen Ortskern weist das unmittelbar vor dem Ersten Weltkrieg errichtete Schulgebäude.
Die Silhouette des Schlosses präsentiert sich in Wernigerode von verschiedenen Standorten immer wieder neu; hier mit dem Agnesberg.

Wernigerode unites tradition and modernity. For 150 years, this popular holiday destination and industrious business centre has offered many tourist attractions and innovative infrastructure. Since 2006, at "Altstadtkreisel" the Harz narrow-gauge railway intersects with today's road traffic: full steam ahead! The pre-1914 schoolhouse faces the nearby town centre.
The Castle's silhouette is visible from various locations in Wernigerode – here, with the Agnesberg.

Seite 8/9: Mehrere Burgen sicherten einst das mittelalterliche Wernigerode. Vom oberen Ende des Zwölfmorgentals im Süden der Altstadt sind die frühere Harburg (links) und das heutige Schloss gut auszumachen.

Seite 10/11: Krippenszene im Hauptaltar der Sylvestrikirche, deren Ursprünge in die Gründungsphase Wernigerodes zurückreichen.

Seite 12/13: Nöschenrode liegt lang gestreckt im Tal des Zillierbachs. Die alte Hörigensiedlung unterhalb des Schlossbergs mauserte sich ab dem ausgehenden 19. Jahrhundert zur attraktiven Vorstadt.

Page 8/9: Several castles once protected mediaeval Wernigerode. From the upper end of the Zwölfmorgental valley at the southern end of the Old Town, the former Harburg Castle (left) and today's Castle are easily visible.

Page 10/11: Crib scene at St Sylvestri Church main altar which originates from the town's founding date.

Page 12/13: Nöschenrode runs along the Zillierbach valley. In the late 19th century, the old Hörigensiedlung settlement below Castle mount rapidly advanced to become an attractive suburb.

Backerei
Einbahnstraße
244

Schöne Ecke

Der Wilde Mann, eine alte Harzer Sagengestalt, wacht seit dem letzten großen Umbau auf Schloss Wernigerode in der zweiten Hälfte des 19. Jahrhunderts über die Weinbergterrassen.

The stone figure of the 'Wild Man' from an old Harz legend keeps watch over terraced vineyards following the latest major rebuilding work at Castle Wernigerode in the second half of the 19th century.

Auf den restaurierten Resten der mittelalterlichen Stadtmauer am Burgberg kann man heute verträumt spazieren. Zu der trutzigen Anlage gehörten einst vier Stadttore und etwa 30 Wachtürme.

A dreamy walk is possible along the restored ruins of the mediaeval town walls at Burgberg. At one time, four gates and about 30 watch towers were part of these defensive ramparts.

Wohin zuerst in Wernigerode? Direkt zum Markt, zum viel bewunderten Rathaus oder gleich hoch hinauf zum Schloss? Erst in die belebte Breite Straße oder lieber auf den Klint, den beschaulichen Hügel, auf dem einst die lokale Geschichte ihren Anfang nahm?

Der Sehenswürdigkeiten gibt es viele in der bunten Stadt am Nordrand des Harzes, und so verteilt sich denn auch die Schar der Gäste in den Straßen und Gassen, in den Galerien und Museen, in den Cafés und auf den Spazierwegen rings um den Ortskern. Kaum zu merken ist's, dass es etwa zwei Millionen Menschen jährlich sind, die Wernigerode für sich entdecken. Und viele kommen wieder.

Tourismus hat hier Tradition. Doch die „curieusen Personen", die seit dem 17. Jahrhundert in zunehmender Zahl auf der Suche nach „seltzamen und denckwürdigen Sachen" den Harz durchstreiften, fanden anfangs wenig Gefallen an der Stadt. Sie besuchten lieber Baumannshöhle und Brocken oder die bekannten Bergwerke des Mittelgebirges. Allenthalben als günstig gelegene Durchgangsstation war Wernigerode den Reisenden ein Begriff. Populärer wurde jene erst ab 1710. Dies allerdings nur, weil der reichsständische und pietistisch gesinnte Graf Christian Ernst zu Stolberg-Wernigerode das hiesige Bergschloss zu seiner festen Residenz auserkoren hatte. Seine Nachfolger taten es ihm gleich, und das war gut für die Stadt. Gäste kamen, den exponiert gelegenen Adelssitz und die dazugehörigen Gärten zu sehen oder die bekannte, schon 1770 mit etwa 30 000 Bänden ausgestattete Bibliothek der gräflichen Familie in Augenschein zu nehmen. Zeitgleich erlebte die Landschaft ringsum ihre romantische Entdeckung. „Die ganze Grafschaft Wernigerode ist ein wahrer Lustgarten", schrieb 1785 Christian Friedrich Schroeder in seiner „Abhandlung vom Brocken und dem übrigen alpinischen Gebürge des Harzes", und er fügte hinzu: „Je näher ihrem Mittelpunkte, der Stadt Wernigerode, je schöner und abwechselnder wird diese einem Garten ähnliche bunte Landschaft."

Bunte Stadt ist Wernigerode seit Beginn des 20. Jahrhunderts. Rund fünfzig Jahre zuvor waren die ersten Sommerfrischler hierher gekommen – in der Hauptsache industrialisierungsgeplagte Großstädter, die sich nach kleinstädtischer Idylle, Natur und Ruhe sehnten und mit ihren Familien auf Wochen oder Monate blieben. Auch ihnen gefiel die liebliche Umgegend am Rande des Harzes, sie aber erkannten gleichzeitig die Reize innerhalb des Gemeinwesens. „Die altersgrauen Stadtmauern und geborstenen Thürme in derselben, sowie die alterthümliche Bauart vieler Gebäude, geben der Stadt ein eigenthümliches interessantes Ansehen", konnte man beispielsweise in einem Reiseführer aus dem Jahre 1859 über Wernigerode lesen. Zugegeben, der Lauf der Zeit ging auch an der mittlerweile preußischen Kreisstadt nicht vorbei. Sie wuchs, wurde modernisiert und industrialisiert, behielt jedoch bei all dem ihre über viele Generationen gewachsene Identität. „Wernigerode ist kein schnell emporgeschossener Kur- und Vergnügungsort ... es ist eine geschichtlich gewordene und in naturgemäßer Weise

Where to go first in Wernigerode? Straight to the market square, its famous Town Hall or to Wernigerode Castle? And how about a stroll along the buzzing Breite Straße? Or maybe to the 'Klint'? – This serene, historic hill where the town was once founded.

A colourful town on the northern edge of the Harz Mountains, Wernigerode is filled with attractions. Crowds of visitors throng the streets and narrow alleys, galleries and museums, or relax in cafés and discover meandering walking routes around the town's centre. Although it's hardly noticeable, Wernigerode welcomes about two million visitors every year. Many people also return.

Tourism has a special tradition here. But in the early days, and since the 17th century, "strangers and inquisitive travellers" who crossed the Harz Mountains in their increasing numbers to find "strange and memorable things" initially found little pleasure in this region. Such travellers preferred to see nearby Baumannshöhle and the Brocken or the famous coal mines of this low-mountain region. Because of its ideal geographical location, Wernigerode was a well-known place to pass through, and gained popularity since 1710. This was thanks to Count Christian Ernst zu Stolberg-Wernigerode, whose sovereign rights and pietistic beliefs guided his choice of the town's hillside castle as the family's permanent residence overlooking the town. The family heirs kept up this tradition, which was beneficial for the town. Visitors arrived to see the prominently situated aristocratic estate with surrounding gardens or to peruse the family's famous library – even in 1770, there were already about 30,000 books. At the same time, the age of Romantic discovery was heralded as visitors came to tour the nearby countryside. "The entire county of Wernigerode is a true pleasure garden", wrote Christian Friedrich Schroeder in 1785 in his "Abhandlung vom Brocken und dem übrigen alpinischen Gebürge des Harzes" ("Tour of Brocken and Other Alpine Peaks of the Harz Mountains"). Moreover, he added: "The closer one draws to the town centre of Wernigerode, the more pleasant and varied the garden, like a colourful landscape."

Wernigerode in the 20th century has become known as the 'colourful town'. Fifty years prior to this, the first summer holidaymakers arrived mainly from the major industrialised cities. The town's newcomers longed to find a provincial idyll, surrounded by nature and tranquillity. Families stayed here for weeks or months. They grew to love the gentle countryside on the edge of the Harz Mountains, while recognising the tensions of community life. "The age-old city walls and their tumbledown turrets, and the antiquated style of many buildings give the town a curious and interesting appearance", was how one travel guide described Wernigerode in 1859. It's true that the signs of progress could no longer pass by this Prussian county town. It was growing, modernising and becoming industrialised, but retained its identity which had evolved over many generations. In 1900, a perceptive and assiduous contemporary chronicler, Dr. Eduard Jacobs, wrote, "Wernigerode is no rapidly emerging spa and leisure town

Schlossbaumeister Karl Frühling hinterließ im letzten Drittel des 19. Jahrhunderts selbst in der Stadt Spuren. Der Neubau des heutigen Gerhart-Hauptmann-Gymnasiums erfolgte nach seinen Plänen.

Karl Frühling, the Castle's master builder, left his mark in town during the last third of the 19th century. Today's Gerhart Hauptmann Grammar School was designed after his plans.

Der Fachwerkstil prägt das architektonische Gesicht Wernigerodes. Diese gekreuzten und geschweiften Rauten aus dem 17. Jahrhundert schmücken die Hausfassade in der Grünen Straße 32.

entwickelte Stadt", schrieb 1900 folgerichtig mit Dr. Eduard Jacobs ein historisch äußerst beflissener Zeitgenosse.

Sieben Jahre später weilte unter tausenden Sommerfrischlern der Schriftsteller und Journalist Hermann Löns in Wernigerode. Sein sechswöchiger Aufenthalt zeigte Langzeitwirkung, veröffentlichte er doch – lebhaft begeistert von Landstrich und Leuten – im Hannoverschen Unterhaltungsblatt vom 30. Mai 1909 eine literarische Plauderei, deren Titel nicht treffender hätte sein können: „Die bunte Stadt am Harz". In Wernigerode selbst erkannte man damals schnell das touristische Potenzial der Formulierung. Ein Jahr verging nur, dann kauften die Verantwortlichen dem Autor kurzerhand die Nutzungsrechte ab. Eine Wernigerode-Werbung ohne Löns' Titel oder Text, das ist seither eher die Ausnahme.

Wernigerode ist reich an Geschichte. Auf den 18. Oktober 1121 datiert die Urkunde, dem der Ort am Zusammenfluss von Zillierbach und Holtemme den Eingang in die schriftlich überlieferte Historie dankt. Wann und wie jener jedoch entstanden ist, lässt sich bis heute nicht zweifelsfrei klären. Archäologische Spuren deuten darauf hin, dass am Klint im 10. Jahrhundert alles begann. Niederungsburg samt kleiner Siedlung – so stellen sich die Fachleute derzeit das Ur-Wernigerode vor.

Unmittelbar an der Kreuzung mehrerer Straßen und Wege gelegen, boten sich den Anwohnern gute Chancen für Handel und Handwerk. Ein Marktflecken entstand. Das begehrte Stadtrecht ließ hingegen etwas auf sich warten, schließlich konnte Wernigerode weder mit einem alten Bischofssitz wie Halberstadt noch mit einer namhaften Kaiserpfalz wie Goslar aufwarten. Doch am 17. April 1229 kamen die Grafen von Wernigerode, seit Beginn des 12. Jahrhunderts mit Herrschaftsrechten in der Gegend betraut, der Bitte der hiesigen Kaufmannschaft nach und verliehen jenen das Privileg, „mit dem die Bürgerschaft von Goslar seit frühen Zeiten ausgezeichnet ist." Städter und Stadtherren profitierten von diesem bedeutsamen Rechtsakt gleichermaßen. Wernigerode wuchs und behauptete sich wirtschaftlich. Die zeittypischen Widrigkeiten wie Epidemien und Fehden bedrohten den Ort, konnten ihm die Lebenskraft dennoch nicht rauben. Als kleines, aber wichtiges Tor zum Harz erlebte Wernigerode mit seinen etwa 2 500 Bewohnern um 1500 den Schritt in die Neuzeit. Dass die Stadt schon damals weit über die Grenzen der Region bekannt war, dokumentiert bis heute ihr früher Eintrag in die von Erhard Etzlaub entworfene und ganz Mitteleuropa abbildende Romwegkarte.

Wernigerode's quaint half-timbered architectural style influences the town's character. Criss-crossed 17th-century timber patterns decorate the main façade at Grüne Straße 32. The same half-timbered pattern also decorates the building at Grüne Straße 32.

Authentische Spuren mittelalterlicher Geschichte in Wernigerode zu finden, erfordert ein gewisses Gespür. Zwar steht am Platze eine Fülle historischer und historisierender Bauten, tatsächlich älter als 500 Jahre sind aber nur wenige. Zu ihnen gehören die Reste der im 13. Jahrhundert angelegten Stadtbefestigung. Wie vielerorts hatte man sie größtenteils in der zweiten Hälfte des 19. Jahrhunderts abgetragen. Nicht ohne Kritik freilich, wie nachstehende Äußerung Dr. Jacobs' illustriert: „So ganz nahe bis an die Schwelle unserer denkmalspflegen-

... the town has evolved in step with history and in an organic way". Seven years later, Hermann Löns, the author and journalist, stayed in Wernigerode along with thousands of summer holidaymakers. His six-week stay had a lasting effect. Profoundly inspired by the countryside and people, the title of his literary causerie – "The colourful town of the Harz Mountains" – could not have been more apt. And in Wernigerode of the time, his slogan rapidly drew in more tourists. After only one year, rights to the author's literary work were quickly purchased. Now, advertising for Wernigerode is never without Löns's text.

Wernigerode verdankt Hermann Löns den werbewirksamen Beinamen „bunte Stadt am Harz". Im Gegenzug errichteten die Städter dem Schriftsteller 1929 auf dem Blockshornberg einen Gedenkstein und benannten die Straße dort oben nach ihm.

Wernigerode has a rich history. The town charter dates from 18 October 1121, and is a written record of the history of the place nestled between the two streams of Zillierbach and Holtemme. However, until today, the town's origins are unknown. Archaeological remains suggest it was originally founded at the 'Klint' in the 10th century. Experts present what was then ancient Wernigerode as Niederungsburg, and also encompassing a small settlement.

At the crossroads of several routes and pathways, the inhabitants had excellent opportunities for trade and handicraft. A market area grew up. The coveted town ordinances, however, took some time to create. Ultimately, Wernigerode could neither wait to be designated an old diocesan town such as Halberstadt nor a renowned imperial seat like Goslar. On 17 April 1229, the Counts of Wernigerode, who were entrusted since the early 12th century with the rights of dominion over this district, accepted the request of local businessmen and granted them the privilege "with which the citizens of Goslar have been invested since the town's early history". The townspeople and rulers profited in equal measure from this important legal ruling. Wernigerode grew and was commercially viable. The typical adversities such as epidemics and feuds threatened the town, yet these could not deprive the place of its vitality. As a small, though important gateway to the Harz Mountains, in about 1500, Wernigerode and its approximately 2,500 townspeople advanced to the modern era. That the city's reputation then already extended far beyond the region's boundaries is documented to this day by its early entry on the Romweg map prepared by Erhard Etzlaub and charting the whole of Central Europe.

Discovering the authentic traces of mediaeval history in Wernigerode is a time-consuming process. The town has many historic buildings, but only some of these are actually more than 500 years old, including the remnants of the town's fortifications dating from the 13th century. As in many places, these were already removed by the second half of the 19th century. The following comment from Dr. Jacobs is illustrative of the critical response: "The town's defences survived intact almost to the modern-day techniques of preserving historical buildings, yet only to fall victim at the last minute to ignorance and misunderstanding." Irrespective of this, in the corner between the Castle mount and the outer defences directly below, two half-open towers with surrounding walls are still visible today – these are typical structures at Wernigerode. The impressively de-

Wernigerode owes its memorable "colourful town in the Harz" slogan to Hermann Löns. In return, the townspeople dedicated a memorial on Blockshornberg, naming the street up here after him.

Der 41 Meter hohe und 1356 erstmals erwähnte Westerntorturm.

The 41-metre Westerntor tower was first mentioned in 1356.

den Zeit hatten sich also die Wehrbauten der Stadt erhalten, um noch im letzten Augenblick blödem Unverstand zum Opfer zu fallen.“ Ungeachtet dessen sind noch heute im Winkel zwischen Burgberg und Vorwerk direkt unterhalb vom Schloss zwei der für Wernigerode typischen Halbschalentürme samt Mauer zu sehen. Auch der beeindruckend trutzige Turm des Westerntores überdauerte die Zeiten, und das obwohl seinem letzten Wächter Heinrich Hotopp bald nach der 1867 verfügten Aufhebung der Torwacht gekündigt worden war.

Mittelalterlichen Ursprungs sind ferner die Kirchen im historischen Wernigerode. Einst gab es derer vier: drei in der Alt- und eine in der Neustadt. Letztere, in der zweiten Hälfte des 13. Jahrhunderts erbaut und Johannis dem Täufer geweiht, bewahrt bis heute am ehesten ihre frühe architektonische Gestalt. Anders die 1230 erstmals erwähnte Sylvestrikirche auf dem Klint und die fünf Jahre später beurkundete Liebfrauenkirche im Burgstraßenviertel. Aus der Vogelperspektive betrachtet sind sie sich ob ihrer neogotischen Türme aus dem ausgehenden 19. Jahrhundert recht ähnlich. Ein Besuch vor Ort offenbart jedoch deutliche Unterschiede. Das Gotteshaus auf dem Gründungshügel der Stadt diente erst als Gemeindekirche und von 1265 bis zur Reformation als Chorherrenstift. Innen und außen Ergebnis mehrerer Umbauetappen, zeigt sich St. Sylvestri heute im Großen und Ganzen so wie 1880 bis 1886 hergerichtet. Die Liebfrauenkirche, die im Spätmittelalter die Funktion der Stadtkirche übernommen hatte, präsentiert sich dagegen in der Gegenwart, abgesehen von ihrem Hauptturm, als geschlossener protestantischer Sakralbau des 18. Jahrhunderts. 1762 eingeweiht, ersetzte er die in einem Großfeuer elf Jahre zuvor zerstörte romanische Vorgängerkirche. Nur der in den Nikolaiplatz eingearbeitete Grundriss sowie ein aufregend moderner Heiliger Nikolaus am Brunnen erinnern an die dritte Wernigeröder Altstadtkirche. Die 1265 zum ersten Mal genannte „ecclesia beati Nicolai“ hatte hier bis zu ihrem Abriss im Jahre 1873 gestanden.

Wernigerode ist Fachwerkstadt. Zugegeben, dies scheint flüchtig betrachtet nichts Besonderes, gibt es doch derer viele in der Region und im ganzen Land. Was also zeichnet die bunte Stadt mit ihrem Fachwerk vor anderen aus? Die Mischung ist's, die Kombination von Fachwerkgebäuden aus sechs Jahrhunderten innerhalb eines Ortskerns, auf engstem Raum. Ständer- und Stockwerkbauten sind erhalten, Häuser im Stil von Renaissance, Barock, Klassizismus und Historismus. Selbst Spätgotik und Jugendstil haben im Wernigeröder Fachwerk ihre Spuren hinterlassen. Kein Zufall also, dass das 95 Hektar umfassende Areal der historischen Altstadt Flächendenkmal ist und die Kommune 1998 Aufnahme in die Deutsche Fachwerkstraße fand.

Katastrophen und deren Überwindung führten hauptsächlich zu jener Architekturmischung. Mehrere Stadtbrände rissen furchtbare Lücken, die jedoch immer wieder in Fachwerk geschlossen wurden. „Häuser, Handlung, Haabe sind verzehret. Gütigster, du hast uns selbst geschlagen. Und was solten wir von Unschuld sagen? Ach wir bekennen: Wir selbst hätten sollen mit verbrennen“,

fiant tower in the western gate also survived intact, even though the last keeper, Heinrich Hotopp, was dismissed soon after the last watch was abolished in 1867.

The churches in historic Wernigerode are also of mediaeval origin. At one time, the town had four in total – three in the Old Town. The church of St John the Baptist in the new town was built in the second half of the 13th century, and has essentially retained its early architectural character to this day. This is not the case for Sylvestri Church on the 'Klint', first mentioned in 1230, and the Church of Our Lady in the Burgstraße district consecrated five years later.

From a bird's eye perspective, the towers of two late 19th-century Neo-Gothic churches seem very similar. But visit each church in turn and you will notice obvious differences. To begin with, the church on the hill where the town originated was used in the early days as a Parish church, and from 1265 to the Reformation, as a friary. The building's interior and exterior were reconstructed at different times. Today, St Sylvestri has largely been restored to its condition of between 1880 and 1886. In the late mediaeval period, the Church of Our Lady was used as the local church, yet apart from the central tower, the main part of this Protestant church dates from the 18th century. Consecrated in 1762, the church replaced the Romanesque building. Eleven years previously it was destroyed in a great fire. Today, the only visible signs of Wernigerode's third church in Old Town are the stones of the original ground plan at Nikolai Square and the beautiful and modern St Nicholas fountain. This is at the site of what, until its demolition in 1873, was originally known in 1265 as "ecclesia beati Nicolai".

At first, Wernigerode's half-timbered houses seem nothing special, given that the buildings are typical of this region. But what makes this colourful town with its half-timbered architecture so attractive is the town centre's varied combination of half-timbered buildings from six centuries and restricted to a confined space. Beam-and-column constructions and multi-storey buildings are preserved alongside houses featuring Renaissance and Baroque structures and neo-classical and historicist buildings. Even traces of Late Gothic and Art Nouveau can be detected in Wernigerode's half-timbered houses. It is no accident that the 95-hectare (235-acre) site of the historic Old Town has become a conservation area, with the municipality being included as a stop on the Deutsche Fachwerkstraße (German Half-Timbered House Road) in 1998.

The combination of architectural styles was mainly an outcome of natural disasters and work to overcome them. Several fires in the town left gaping voids which were constantly filled by adding more half-timbered buildings. "Homes, livelihoods and possessions are destroyed. Dear God, you have hit us yourself. And what are we to say of innocence? Alas, we confess: we should ourselves have been consumed by the fire", wrote a shocked Christoph Gottfried Jacobi at the sight of the great fire raging "on the 30th June, 1751, at about 11 o'clock in the morning until early next morning in Wernigerode Old Town, and turning more than three hundred buildings to rubble." The flames had engulfed two

Der Halbschalenturm in der Stadtmauer am Burgberg.

The half-open tower in the town wall at Burgberg.

Pure Lebensfreude versprüht diese Kinderplastik im Brunnenhof direkt an der Breiten Straße. Entlang der schon 1399 als „Bredestrate" erwähnten Einkaufsmeile erwarten ganz unterschiedlich gestaltete Höfe ihre Besucher.

schrieb der betroffene Christoph Gottfried Jacobi unter dem Eindruck des Großfeuers, das „den 30ten Junii 1751. Mittags gegen 11. Uhr, bis des andern Morgens frühe in der Altstadt Wernigerode mehr als dreihundert Gebäude in die Asche legte". Zwei Drittel aller Wohnhäuser sowie die Liebfrauenkirche fielen damals den Flammen zum Opfer. Den größten Brand ihrer Geschichte hatte die Stadt schon im August 1528 erlebt. 470 von 554 Gebäuden waren damals vernichtet worden. Ein letztes Großfeuer ereilte Wernigerode dann ausgerechnet in dem gesamteuropäischen „Hunger- und Kummerjahr" 1847. Der amtliche Bericht bezifferte „die Zahl der sämmtlichen, völlig abgebrannten Gebäude" auf 403, darunter 149 Wohnhäuser und 251 Neben- und Hintergebäude. Abermals wurde das betroffene Quartier in Fachwerk aufgebaut.

Relativ geschlossene Architekturensemble sind heute vor allem dort zu sehen, wo die ausgedehnten Brände der Jahre 1751 und 1847 gewütet hatten: im Burgstraßenviertel rings um die Liebfrauenkirche bzw. auf der Heide, zwischen Western- und Hinterstraße. Aber selbst außerhalb der engen Altstadtgrenzen und besonders in den 1907 bzw. 1929 eingemeindeten Ortsteilen Hasserode und Nöschenrode wirkt die Gestaltung vieler Fachwerkhäuser recht homogen. Im ausgehenden 19. oder im beginnenden 20. Jahrhundert gänzlich neu entworfen, zeigen die Fassaden hier alle Spielarten des Historismus.

Besagte Brände sind ebenfalls Ursache dafür, dass sehr alte Gebäude in Wernigerode eher selten anzutreffen sind. Auf dem Klint haben sich jedoch wie am Markt und in dessen unmittelbarer Nähe sowie in der Breiten Straße einige Einzeldenkmale erhalten, die es lohnt, genauer zu betrachten. Im Schatten der Sylvestrikirche steht auf dem Oberpfarrkirchhof zum Beispiel das Gadenstedtsche Haus von 1582 mit einem reich verzierten Hochrenaissance-Erker. Ums Eck sind hier zudem mit den Hausnummern 10 und 11 zwei eher unauffällige Fachwerkhäuser aus dem letzten Drittel des 16. Jahrhunderts zu sehen. Auch einige der Gebäude um den sogenannten Kunsthof in der Marktstraße 1 und 3 entstammen jener Zeit, so die 1556 errichtete und innen wie außen seit den 1980er Jahren sorgsam restaurierte Kemenate des Bürgermeisters Thomas Schütze und dessen Frau Anna Plathner. Bereits unmittelbar nach dem 1528er Stadtbrand wurden die sogenannte Remise und Teile der „Galerie 1530" gebaut. Am Markt selbst stehen das Rathaus und das Gothische Haus für jahrhundertealte Fachwerktradition. In der Breiten Straße schließlich lockt, nur einen Steinwurf vom Marktplatz entfernt, das Café Wien. Im Kern ein Fachwerkhaus von 1583 kam es 1897 in den Besitz des Konditormeisters Hauer. Der wurde seinem Namen wahrhaft gerecht und gestaltete es mit großem Schwung, aber leider ohne das nötige denkmalpflegerische Fingerspitzengefühl um; nichts blieb

Pure joie de vivre radiates from this sculpture of children at Brunnenhof, directly on Breite Straße. Along "Bredestrate", already designated as a shopping district in 1399, visitors can expect a variety of different courtyards.

Im Angerzentrum am östlichen Ende der Breiten Straße.

thirds of all residential houses and the Church of Our Lady. But the town's biggest disaster caused by fire occurred in August 1528 when 470 out of a total of 554 buildings were destroyed. The last great fire took hold in Wernigerode in 1847, the year of suffering and the Great Famine across Europe. The official report estimated that "the number of all buildings totally burned down" was 403, including 149 residential houses and 251 annexes and rear buildings. But again, half-timbered buildings were rebuilt in this quarter.

Nowadays, especially where the great fires of 1751 and 1847 did the most damage, the buildings are grouped in a relatively tight ensemble: in the Burgstraße district around the Church of Our Lady or on the moor between Western- and Hinterstrasse. Even beyond the Old Town's limits and especially in the Hasserode and Nöschenrode districts, established between 1907 and 1929, many half-timbered houses are designed to appear homogeneous. Having undergone a complete redesign in the 19th or early 20th centuries, all of the façades here show historicist features.

The aftermath of the great fires also explains why so few of Wernigerode's very old buildings are intact. On the 'Klint', however, in the market square, immediately adjacent, and on Breite Straße, several listed buildings are preserved, which are worthwhile considering in greater detail. In the shadow of St Sylvestri Church at the high Parish churchyard (Oberpfarrkirchhof), for example, you will find the 'Gadenstedtsches Haus' dating from 1582 and with an ornate High Renaissance bay-gable. Around the corner, at numbers 10 and 11, there are also two rather inconspicuous half-timbered houses dating from the last third of the 16th century. Several of the buildings in Kunsthof courtyard at Marktstraße 1 and 3 date from this period, for instance, the mayor's residence, where Thomas Schütze, the Mayor of Wernigerode, and his wife, Anna Plathner, lived and which originates from 1556. It was renovated inside and outside during the 1980s. The so-called Remise and parts of "Galerie 1530" were constructed immediately after the 1528 town fire. The Town Hall and 'Gothisches Haus', located in the market square, are prominent examples of the town's tradition in half-timbered work. Finally, Café Wien at Breite Straße is just a stone's throw from the market square. In 1897, its traditional half-timbered 1583 building was owned by the master confectioner, Hauer. Living up to his name ('hauen' literally means to quarry), his building plans were produced with great élan, though unfortunately they lacked the required treatment in sympathy with a listed building. Therefore, the older, lower floors were not preserved, although the locals will never forget that Hauer laid the foundation stone of the town's most comfortable coffee house.

At Anger centre, at the eastern end of Breite Straße.

At the new end of Breite Straße, two newcomers to the town were to leave behind especially impressive half-timbered buildings. The blacksmith, Michael Krell of Swabia, built the Krell Forge in 1678 – look out for the characteristic cross-hatched pattern which is reminiscent of his Upper German homeland. Heinrich Krummel, the rich corn dealer from Berlin, had rather different ideas. Four years previously, he built the residential and commercial building out of

Oben: Wappen der Grafen zu Stolberg-Wernigerode am Rathausportal.
Unten: Wasserspeier des Wohltäterbrunnens auf dem Markt.

Above: Coat-of-arms of the Counts Stolberg-Wernigerode at the town hall portal.
Below: Wohltäterbrunnen fountain, gargolye in the market square.

so zum Beispiel von den beiden alten Untergeschossen. Dennoch legte Hauer, und das vergessen ihm die Wernigeröder nie, den Grundstein für das gemütlichste Kaffeehaus der Stadt.

Ausgerechnet zwei Zugezogene waren es, die im neustädtischen Teil der Breiten Straße besonders eindrucksvolle Fachwerkbauten hinterließen. Grobschmied Michael Krell aus Schwaben baute 1678 die Krellsche Schmiede mit ihren charakteristischen gekreuzten und geschweiften Rauten, einer Reminiszenz an seine oberdeutsche Heimat. Anders der reiche Kornhändler Heinrich Krummel aus Berlin. Das von ihm vier Jahre zuvor errichtete Wohn- und Geschäftshaus scheint mehr Holzrelief denn Fachwerkhaus. Kein Balken, der da nicht verziert, kein Brüstungsfeld, das ob seiner Bilder nicht jeden Betrachter in seinen Bann zieht.

Zier der Stadt und Stolz der Bürger ist das Rathaus. 1277 erstmals beurkundet, begann es seine Vita als Spelhus, als Gemeindehaus. Ursprünglich Eigentum der Grafen von Wernigerode schenkte es deren letzter Vertreter zwei Jahre vor seinem Tod 1427 der Stadt. Nicht lange, dann legten die Bürger los, bauten um und aus. So wartete denn das Gebäude schon im ausgehenden 15. Jahrhundert im Wesentlichen mit dem Antlitz auf, das uns heute gut vertraut ist: steinerner Unterbau, repräsentativer Fachwerkaufsatz und natürlich die passenden schlanken Erkertürme. Rathaus war das Gebäude damals aber noch immer nicht. Erst einige Jahre nachdem das Feuer von 1528 an der Ostseite des Marktes den alten Ratssitz verwüstet hatte, änderte sich dies. Und wieder wurde erweitert und ergänzt. Auch die Folgejahrhunderte hinterließen ihre architektonischen Spuren am Rathaus, speziell aber die Jahre zwischen 1936 und 1939. Seinerzeit entstand aus dem historisch gewachsenen Gebäudekomplex ein regelrechtes Rathausviertel. Das alte Waaghaus aus dem 16. Jahrhundert verlängerte man um das Doppelte, hinzu kamen das im traditionellen Fachwerk aufgeführte Sparkassengebäude sowie ein mehrgeschossiger Flügel zum Klint hin. Stadtbaurat und Provinzkonservator arbeiteten damals Hand in Hand; die wertvolle überkommene Bausubstanz wurde folglich geschont und so harmonisch mit dem Angefügten verbunden, dass es bis heute schwerfällt, spontan Alt und Neu sicher zu unterscheiden. Was seine gegenwärtige Nutzung anbelangt, setzt man im Rathaus ganz auf Tradition: in ihm wird getraut und gefeiert, beraten und beschlossen, gehandelt und mitunter auch gespielt. Wie heißt es doch in dem alten Spruch über dem Hauptportal? „Einer acht's, der andre betracht's, der dritte verlacht's, was macht's."

Und schließlich das Schloss. Reisebuchautor Wilhelm Gröning bezeichnete es 1850 als „die Krone des ganzen Harzgaus", während Verfasserkollege Gustav Adolf Leibrock zwanzig Jahre später von einer „der schönsten Perlen im Diademe des Harzes" sprach. Selbst „Wartburg des Harzes" wurde Schloss Wernigerode schon genannt, und der Komplimente wären noch weitere hinzuzufügen.

what seems more timber-relief than half-timbered work. Each beam is ornately decorated, and the balustrades cannot fail to enchant the viewer who will surrender to its spellbinding and picturesque image.

Wernigerode Town Hall is the pride and joy of its citizens. First registered in 1277, it started out as the 'Spelhus', or town's parish hall. Originally owned by Count von Wernigerode, the building's final owner donated it to the town two years prior to his death in 1427. Not long afterwards, residents began renovating and extending the building. At the end of the 15th century, the building was essentially what we are familiar with today: stone substructure, representative half-timbered upper section and, of course, suitably fine gabled turrets. At that time, the building did not yet serve as a Town Hall. This did not change until the edifice was extended and renovated several years after the 1528 fire destroyed the old Town Hall. The building's architecture can also be traced in subsequent centuries, too, especially from 1936 to 1939. In its day, the historical complex formed a district in its own right, spreading out from the Town Hall.

The old 16th-century Weighing House was doubled in length and the traditional half-timber design of the savings bank as well as a multi-storey wing were added towards the 'Klint'. In those days, the planning director and curator of the province worked hand in hand. Valuable traditional buildings were therefore protected and harmoniously adjoined to the more modern building sections. Until today, it is difficult to tell for certain what is old and new. As far as its present use is concerned, tradition took precedence in the Town Hall: weddings and festivities take place here, people debate and take decisions, do business and, occasionally, take part in games. Take a look at the old saying above the main entrance: "Einer acht's, der andre betracht's, der dritte verlacht's, was macht's" ('One person respects, the other regards it, a third breaks into laughter – what does it matter?')

Last but not least, there is Wernigerode Castle, which travel writer Wilhelm Gröning described in 1850 as "the jewel of all Harz". Twenty years later, a colleague and author, Gustav Adolf Leibrock, referred to one of "the most beautiful pearls in the diadem of the Harz Mountains". Wernigerode Castle was even known as the "Wartburg of the Harz" and more praise could be added. The Castle sits 120 metres high above the town centre and is situated on a spur of Agnes Mountain, previously known as Biegenberg. The history books record that the castle dates as far back as 1213. About a hundred years previously, Count von Wernigerode, who was regarded as among the most powerful men of the Harz region, founded the "castrum". The Castle became the family seat – a clever choice, since the castle was already regarded as especially secure in 1223. It maintained this reputation and was further expanded and extended until the early modern period. After 1626, the fortifications – from now on in the ownership of Count zu Stolberg for almost two hundred years – were recorded

Oben: Am Klintstein begann im 10. Jahrhundert angeblich der Aufbau Wernigerodes. Unten: Historistischer Wasserspeier im Innenhof des Schlosses.

Above: Wernigerode was thought to have been established in the 10th century at the 'Klint' stone. Below: Historicist gargolye in the Castle interior.

Neben der architektonischen Gesamtkomposition von Alt und Neu trugen zahlreiche phantasievolle Fabelwesen, wie hier auf dem Kamin im Festsaal, im Detail dazu bei, dass der in seinen Fundamenten mittelalterliche Herrschaftssitz über den Dächern der Stadt seit dem Umbau im 19. Jahrhundert als Märchenschloss gilt.

Old and new create a complete composition in architectural terms. Numerous mythical figures – such as the detail shown here on the chimneypiece in the ballroom – also mean that this mediaeval castle is visible over the rooftops. Since the 19th-century reconstruction, this is regarded as a fairytale Castle.

120 Meter über dem Zentrum der Stadt, auf einem Sporn des Agnesberges, der früher den Namen Biegenberg trug, erhebt sich das Schloss. Seine schriftlich überlieferte Geschichte reicht bis 1213 zurück. Etwa einhundert Jahre zuvor war das „castrum" durch die Grafen von Wernigerode begründet worden. Jene zählten zu den mächtigsten Herren des Harzes und nahmen ihren Stammsitz hier. Eine kluge Entscheidung, galt die Burg doch schon 1223 als besonders fest. Diesen Ruf behielt sie, weiter und weiter ausgebaut, bis in die frühe Neuzeit. Noch 1626 taucht die Wehranlage – nunmehr knapp zweihundert Jahre im Besitz der Grafen zu Stolberg – in den Annalen als „Frontir", also als Festung auf. Ihrer militärischen Karriere setzte schließlich die zunehmende Kraft der mauerbrechenden Feuerwaffen in den stürmischen Zeiten des Dreißigjährigen Krieges ein Ende. Neuer Glanz zog erst im 18. Jahrhundert in die alten Mauern ein, als die Stolberger in ihnen dauerhaft Hof und Residenz hielten. Sie taten dies bis in das 20. Jahrhundert hinein.

„Dieser Schloßbau ist ein Geschenk des Fürsten und seines Baumeisters an den Harz und alle dessen Besucher, das will so ziemlich sagen: an ganz Norddeutschland, und ein edles Denkmal, das sich das letzte der alten Harzgrafengeschlechter selber gesetzt hat." Jener Fürst, von dem der Schriftsteller Hans Hoffmann 1899 schrieb, ist der bekannteste Stolberger: der 1890 in den Reichsfürstenstand erhobene Graf Otto. Für den erfolgreichen Unternehmer und bedeutenden Politiker der Bismarckära und seine hochadelige Familie war standesgemäße Repräsentation ein gesellschaftliches Muss. So ging er denn 1862 daran, ausgewählte Räume seines Schlosses zu renovieren. Bis 1885 wurde der alte Adelssitz grundsätzlich neu gestaltet. Unter maßgeblicher Leitung des Architekten Karl Frühling entstand in jenen Jahren das Märchenschloss, für das Wernigerode heute so bekannt ist. Als historistisches Gesamtkunstwerk bezeichnen es die Fachleute eingedenk der umgebenden Landschaft, der Terrassen sowie Gärten. Und sie loben in diesem Zusammenhang das Geschick von Bauherr und Baumeister, überkommene historische Substanz gekonnt mit seinerzeit modernen historisierenden Elementen zu einem beeindruckenden Ganzen verknüpft zu haben.

Selbst in unseren Tagen lässt sich's gut eintauchen in die glänzende Epoche, da auf Schloss Wernigerode Grafen, Fürsten und selbst Könige und Kaiser zu Besuch weilten. Knapp fünfzig Räume stehen zur Besichtigung offen, und viele davon präsentieren sich wie zu Graf Ottos Zeiten. Nicht von ungefähr ist das Museum mit seinen etwa 180 000 Gästen pro Jahr das meistbesuchte in Sachsen-Anhalt und in der Harzregion.

Wohin zuerst in Wernigerode? Direkt in die Stadt oder erst in die nähere Umgebung? Ins romantische Tal der Steinernen Renne, auf den Kaiserturm, in die beschaulichen Laubwälder rings um den Ort, in die raue Wildnis des Nationalparks Harz oder mit der Harzquer- und Brockenbahn auf den höchsten Gipfel des Gebirges? Nein, auf den Agnesberg, der mit 389 m üNN das Schloss knapp

in the archives as "frontir", or as a fortress. The end of its military use came with the increasing power of explosive weaponry during the turbulence of the Thirty Years' War. Only in the 18th century did the old walls radiate a new resplendence when the Stolberg family were in permanent residence and held court here. They continued to do so until the 20th century.

"This castle construction is a gift of the Prince and his master builder to the Harz region and to all its visitors, that is to say – to the whole of northern Germany; it stands as an erudite monument, established by the last of the old aristocratic dynasties in the Harz region." Hans Hoffmann referred in 1899 to the Prince as the best-known member of the Stolberg family and in 1890 Count Otto rose to the status of Imperial Prince. As a successful businessman and leading politician of the Bismarck era, it was important for the Count's aristocratic family to live in a manner that accorded with the family's social rank and status. In 1862, the count set about renovating selected rooms in his castle, and by 1885 the family residence was entirely renovated and basically redesigned. Under the directorship of architect Karl Frühling, during these years, the fairytale castle was created for which Wernigerode is so famous today. Experts refer to the Castle as a historicist Gesamtkunstwerk (complete artwork) in view of the surrounding landscape, terraces and gardens. The skilled master builders and developers earned praise in their abilities to combine antiquated historic buildings with historicist elements, which were considered modern in their day, and to create an impressive building ensemble.

Even now, it is easy to immerse oneself in the glorious era, when counts, princes and even kings and emperors visited and stayed at Wernigerode Castle. Almost fifty rooms are open to the public, and many are kept as they were in Count Otto's lifetime. It is no accident that the museum attracts 180,000 visitors every year – this is Saxony-Anhalt's and the Harz Region's most pupolar museum.

Wernigerode – there are so many places to visit first – walk straight into town or explore the nearby countryside. Venture into the wildly Romantic 'Steinerne Renne' valley, or climb up to Kaiserturm tower or explore tranquil, leafy woodlands surrounding the town and the unspoilt wilderness of Harz National Park. Or equally, take a ride on the trans-Harz and Brocken railway up to the highest mountain peak. Climb up to Agnesberg, towering above the Castle at a height of 389 metres above sea level. From here, visitors enjoy a panoramic view of the historic Stolberg residence, of Wernigerode, Nöschenrode and Hasserode, and an unimpeded view of the sprawling and opening Holtemme valley in the west, of the peaks and mountains of the Harz and the Old Man, Brocken.

From up here, the wind gently rustles through the leaves, a bird sings and, from the plain, the busy hum of the town is just audible. On Agnesberg, you can while away the hours in dreamy reminiscence, hatch plans or enjoy the moment. What view could be more captivating?

Selbst Gräfin Anna zu Stolberg-Wernigerode steuerte ihre Ideen zur historistischen Wandlung des Barockschlosses bei. Der von ihr entworfene Zwerg mit dem traditionsreichen Stolberger Hirsch auf dem Wappenschild behauptet seinen Platz am Aufgang zum Rauchsalon in der Halle.

Countess Anna zu Stolberg-Wernigerode also presented ideas for the historicist transformation of the Baroque castle. Her design for a dwarf with the traditional Stolberg stag on the coat-of-arms boldly maintains its position on the staircase to the smokers' salon in the hall.

überragt. Er gibt seinen Besuchern den Blick frei auf das geschichtsträchtige Residenzhaus der Stolberger, auf Wernigerode, Nöschenrode und Hasserode; gewährt Sicht in das breit ausladende und sich im Westen verjüngende Tal der Holtemme, auf die Höhen und Klippen des Harzes und auf Vater Brocken.

Der Wind fährt hier oben leise durch die Blätter, ein Vogel meldet sich, und aus der Ebene steigt ein leises Rauschen der städtischen Klänge empor. Auf dem Agnesberg kann man träumend sich erinnern, Pläne schmieden oder einfach nur den Augenblick genießen. Kann eine Aussicht schöner sein?

Seite 28: Die zwischen 1869 und 1872 errichtete Freiterrasse besitzt eine stolze Höhe von 24 Metern. In den Jahren von 1998 bis 2006 wurde sie nach alten Vorlagen aufwendig restauriert.

Page 28: The open terrace, built between 1869 and 1872, stands at a proud elevation of 24 metres. From 1998 to 2006, the terrace was restored according to old plans.

Rings um den 395 Meter hohen Agnesberg erstreckt sich der einstige fürstliche Tiergarten.

The once princely zoo stretches for 395 metres around Agnesberg peak.

Wernigerode schmiegt sich unmittelbar an die nordöstlichen Ausläufer des Harzes, dessen Höhen in der nahen Umgebung bis zu 400 m üNN erreichen. Der historische Ortskern selbst liegt auf 240 m üNN und wird von den beiden schlanken neogotischen Türmen der Liebfrauenkirche (links) und der Sylvestrikirche (rechts) sowie von der prächtigen Silhouette des Bergschlosses beherrscht.

Wernigerode is located close to the north-eastern extension of the Harz Mountains with peaks close by reaching 400 above sea level. The historic town centre is 240 m above sea level and dominated by two slender neo-Gothic towers of the Church of Our Lady (left) and Sylvestri Church (right) as well as the magnificent silhouette of the Castle on the hill.

Für die wechselvolle Geschichte des Rathauses stehen unter anderem die 33 Knaggenfiguren, von denen jene an der dem Gothischen Haus zugewandten Seite (Fotos) sowie an der Hauptfassade seit über 500 Jahren an ihrem Platze sind. Aus den 1930er Jahren stammen die Plastiken an der Ostseite des Rathauses. Der Wernigeröder Holzbildhauer Otto Welte erinnert mit ihnen an typische Handwerksberufe.

The town hall's chequered history is revealed, among other things, by the 33 wood sculpture figures – those on the façade facing the 'Gothisches Haus' (photos) and on the main façade have stood here for over 500 years. The sculptures on the eastern side of the town hall date from the 1930s. Local Wernigerode wood sculptor, Otto Welte's figures represent typical handcraft skills.

Der Wernigeröder Weihnachtsmarkt gehört ob seiner romantischen Kulisse zu den beliebtesten der Region. Im Dezember 2008 konnten die Besucher direkt vor dem Rathaus den 3,65 Meter hohen sowie 180 Kilogramm schweren und damit seinerzeit größten Schokoladenweihnachtsmann der Welt bewundern (unten).

Wernigerode Christmas market is among the most popular in this region due to its romantic backdrop. In December 2008, right in front of the town hall, visitors marvelled at a chocolate Santa measuring 3.65 metres in height and weighing in at 180 kilograms – then, the world's largest Santa Claus! (below).

Quirliges Treiben in der Fußgängerzone ist im Sommer alltäglich. Stimmungsvolle Feste, wie das Rathausfest und die Neustadter Weintage mit den Winzern aus der Pfälzer Partnerstadt, locken zusätzlich viele Gäste an.

Every day in summer, the pedestrian zone is buzzing with life. Jovial fests such as those at the Town Hall and Neustadt Wine Festival with vintners from Wernigerode's twin town attract many more visitors.

Gothisches Haus

Seit der zweiten Hälfte des 15. Jahrhunderts behauptet das Gothische Haus seinen Platz neben dem Rathaus. Der einstige Wohnsitz reicher Bürger, der früher „dat Grote Hus am Market“ genannt wurde, beherbergte ab 1848 eine Schankwirtschaft.
Die Außenfassade des heutigen stilvollen Hotels schmücken Nachbildungen spätmittelalterlicher Knaggen (links), deren Originale im Inneren zu sehen sind.

Since the second half of the 15th century, the ‘Gothisches Haus’ has stood alongside the Town Hall. This former residence of wealthy citizens went by the name of “dat Grote Hus am Market” and was a tavern from 1848.
The exterior of today’s elegant hotel is decorated with late mediaeval wood sculptures (left) – the originals are exhibited inside.

Wiecker
Conditorei Café Catering
Familientradition Wiecker
in Wernigerode seit 1636

Rings um den Markt laden Cafés und Gasthäuser ein. Zu den ältesten Hotels gehört der 1760 erstmals erwähnte „Weiße Hirsch“ (oben). Der 1848 auf dem Platz errichtete neogotische Brunnen erinnert an Menschen, die sich um die Stadt besonders verdient gemacht haben.
Modernere Brunnen, wie in der oberen Breiten Straße (rechts), gibt es einige. Die Pfälzer Elwetritsche (unten) verzaubert jenen auf dem Neuen Markt.

Cafés and guesthouses surround the market square. The “Weiße Hirsch” (above) is one of the oldest hotels and was first listed in 1760. The neo-Gothic fountain positioned at the market square in 1848 is dedicated to all those who offered their services for the town.
There are a number of more contemporary fountains, for instance, at upper Breite Straße (right). The bird of the Palatinate “Elwetritsche” (left) adorns the fountain at Neuer Markt.

Abwechslungsreiche Fotomotive bietet die Innenstadt mit dem Glockenspiel in der Westernstraße sowie mit den Fächerrosetten an der Kemenate und dem Kunsthof in der Marktstraße 1.
Im 16. Jahrhundert ließ sich Bürgermeister Thomas Schütze diese Kemenate als „gute Stube" errichten. In deren Innenräumen (Seite 44) haben sich zum Teil originale Renaissancewandmalereien erhalten.

In the centre downtown, the chimes on Westernstraße and ornamental fan rosettes at the mayor's residence and the 'Kunsthof' art courtyard at Marktstraße 1 offer plenty of photo opportunities.
In the 16th century, Thomas Schütze, the mayor used this house as a "parlour reception room" – the interior rooms (page 44) still feature some of the Renaissance wall murals.

Kunst zum Anfassen in der Marktstraße: „Die Turmschnecke" von Gernot Rumpf.

"Hands on art" at Marktstraße: "the tower snail" by Gernot Rumpf.

Die bald 800 Jahre alte Sylvestrikirche (links) auf dem Gründungshügel von Wernigerode. In der Sakristei des Gotteshauses sind wertvolle Schätze ausgestellt wie das Magdalenentuch aus der Mitte des 13. Jahrhunderts und der filigrane spätgotische Altar der Georgskapelle (Mittelteil, oben).

The old Sylvestri Church (left), which will soon be 800 years old, at the hill where Wernigerode was founded. In the church registry, valuable treasures are exhibited such as the Magdelene cloth dating from the mid-13th century and the filigree late-Gothic altar of George's Chapel (centrepiece, above).

Im Kirchenschiff der Sylvestrikirche befinden sich unter anderem ein Segen spendender Christus aus der Zeit um 1500 und ein gotischer Eichenschrank aus dem 13. Jahrhundert.

Positioned in the nave of Sylvestri Church are, among other things, Christ offering blessings dating from about 1500, and a Gothic oak cupboard from the 13th century.

Seite 49: Der von dem Brüsseler Meister Arnold im ausgehenden 15. Jahrhundert gearbeitete Altar beherrscht den Chorraum von St. Sylvestri. Im Zentrum des geschnitzten und reich vergoldeten Mittelschreins stehen die Geburt Jesu sowie der Zug der Heiligen Drei Könige.

Page 49: The altarpiece worked by Master Arnold from Brussels in the late 15th century dominates the choir of St Sylvestri. The birth of Christ and arrival of the Three Kings are at the centre of the carved and rich giltwork of the middle altar section.

INRI

Der stolze Ritter Asche von Kram, dies verrät die Inschrift an seinem Grabmal, verstarb 1567 dreiundvierzigjährig und hatte vierzehn Jahre mit „SEINER LIBEN HAVSFRAVEN ANNA VON VELTHEIM GOTSELIG IM EHE STANDT" gelebt.

Seite 50: Blick in die Sakristei der Sylvestrikirche (links). Die kunstvoll geschnitzte Heilige Barbara mit dem Turm (rechts) hat ihren Platz in der Predella des Hauptaltars. Mehrere Grabdenkmäler aus dem 16. und 17. Jahrhundert zieren, wie auch das Epitaph des 1586 verstorbenen Schlosshauptmanns Dietrich von Gadenstedt (unten), das Innere von St. Sylvestri.

The resplendent knight, Asche von Kram, as described on the gravestone inscription, died in 1567 at the age of forty-three and lived for fourteen years with "HIS DEAR WIFE, ANNA VON VELTHEIM, WITH GOD'S BLESSING IN THE UNION OF MARRIAGE".

Page 50: View of the registry at St Sylvestri Church (left). The artfully carved St Barbara with tower (right) occupies her place on the predella of the main altarpiece. Several 16th and 17th-century gravestones are inside St Sylvestri including the epitaph for Dietrich von Gadenstedt (below), the Captain of the Castle, who died in 1586.

Auf dem Klint, unmittelbar hinter dem Rathaus, hat das Harzmuseum sein Domizil. In einem klassizistischen Fachwerkhaus aus dem Jahre 1821 werden hier Geschichte und Kultur sowie Flora und Fauna der Region präsentiert.
Zu den Exponaten der nach umfangreichen Sanierungsarbeiten 2001 eröffneten neuen Dauerausstellung gehört dieser 1817 im Harz erlegte Luchs. Freunden der Harzkunst steht seit 2006 im Harzmuseum ein thematisches Schaudepot offen.

Harz Museum is located on the 'Klint' immediately behind the town hall. The region's history, culture as well as flora and fauna are on display in this neo-classical half-timbered building dating from 1821.
After extensive renovation work in 2001, the new permanent exhibition includes this lynx, preserved in resin in 1817. Art enthusiasts will enjoy a themed section of the exhibition which has been on display in the Harz Museum since 2006.

Einst stand auch das im ausgehenden 17. Jahrhundert errichtete Schiefe Haus in der Klintgasse im Lot. Der stete Strom des Wassergrabens, der die im Haus arbeitende Mühle trieb, unterspülte jedoch deren Fundament und sorgte so für die heute beeindruckende Schräglage.

Seite 54: Architekturmix am Ende der Westernstraße (oben): Das historistische Gebäude des ehemaligen fürstlichen Gymnasiums (rechts), das neue Parkhaus des Gothischen Hauses und die Sylvestrikirche.
Kleine Fachwerkhäuser unterschiedlicher Bauetappen blieben in der Hinterstraße des Heideviertels erhalten (unten).

The 'Crooked House' dating from the late 17th century once stood in Klintgasse. The steady flow of the water in the moat, which powered the mill working in the building, undermined the foundation, thus causing the building's impressive slant.

Page 54: Diverse architecture at the end of Westernstraße (above): the historicist building of the former princely grammar school (right), the new car park at 'Gothisches Haus' and St Sylvestri Church.
Small half-timbered buildings from different epochs are preserved in the back streets of the Heide district (below).

Am Ende der Marktstraße gegenüber dem aus originalen Fundamentsteinen nachempfundenen Grundriss des 1967 abgerissenen Dullenturms animiert Jo Jastrams Plastik „Die Rast“ zum Pausieren und zum nonverbalen Kommunizieren.
Handwerker und Tagelöhner lebten früher in den sogenannten Buden in der Kochstraße (rechts). Das Kleinste Haus der Stadt, noch bis 1976 als Wohnung dienend, kann heute besichtigt werden.

At the end of Marktstraße, opposite the original foundation stone modelled on the site of the tower demolished in 1967, Jo Jastram's sculpture "The Rest" attracts people to take a break and communicate – non-verbally.
Craftsmen and day labourers previously lived in the so-called booths on Kochstraße (right). The town's smallest house, which was still lived in until 1976, is now open to the public.

Ferienhaus
Kochstraße

Allein der Verlauf der Häuserzeilen und Straßenzüge auf dem 1362 zum ersten Mal in einem Schriftdokument benannten Klint sowie die von Archäologen hier geborgenen Funde lassen den Schluss zu, dass die Ortsgeschichte auf diesem Hügel im 10. Jahrhundert begann. Eine Niederungsburg, die noch im Jahre 1544 von Wall und Graben gesäumte „Schnavenburg", beherrschte ursprünglich den Platz. In unmittelbarer Nähe soll in ottonischer Zeit zudem eine Kapelle gestanden haben, der Vorgängerbau der Sylvestrikirche. Vom Ur-Wernigerode des Mittelalters ist wenig erhalten geblieben. Verheerende Brände legten die Stadt mehrfach in Schutt und Asche. Doch die Bewohner ließen sich nicht entmutigen und bauten wieder und wieder auf. Wer Spuren des ganz alten Wernigerode sucht, mag die Klintgasse durchschreiten. Alles andere als geradlinig und nur gut zwei Meter breit, bewahrt sie als einzige Gasse der Stadt ihr frühneuzeitliches Flair.

The alignment of the buildings and street patterns on the 'Klint', which was first recorded in 1362, and archaeological finds suggest that the town's history began on this very hill in the 10th century. A lowland castle, the Schnavenburg, originally dominated the square. In 1544, this castle was still surrounded by ramparts and a moat. In Otto's time, a chapel is supposed to have stood nearby – the forerunner of St Sylvestri Church. Little remains of early mediaeval Wernigerode. Devastating fires razed the town to the ground – several times. But the citizens were not downhearted, rebuilding time after time. Visitors discovering traces of old Wernigerode should cross Klintgasse – a narrow alley, anything but straight and only about two metres wide. This is the only alley in the town to retain something of the town's early-modern character.

Am Oberpfarrkirchhof auf dem Klint blieb unmittelbar neben der Sylvestrikirche ums Eck eine sehenswerte Fachwerkzeile erhalten. Die beiden Gebäude Nummer 10 und 11, das belegen jüngste Holzuntersuchungen, sind frühestens im Jahre 1579 errichtet worden und gehörten zusammen. Sein besonderes Gesicht verdankt das Doppelhaus der deutlichen Vorkragung des Obergeschosses, den zu Rollen gearbeiteten Balkenköpfen sowie den tief herausgeschnitzten Schiffskehlen an den Saumschwellen bzw. Füllhölzern. Beim genauen Hinsehen lassen sich an den Fassaden neben einigen jahrhundertealten Abbundzeichen auch kleine Palmetten und Sterne entdecken.

A row of half-timbered houses is worth looking at on the 'Klint', at the high Parish churchyard, directly next to St Sylvestri Church and around the corner. Both numbers 10 and 11, as recently documented by age tests on the timber, were constructed at the earliest in 1579 and were adjoined. The duplex building retains its special character thanks to the obvious projection of upper floor, scrollwork on the beam heads and the ship's coving on the girt beams. Look closer and you will spot several century-old signs on the beams, with small palms and stars.

13
HAUS·GADENSTEDE·

Durchblick vom Gadenstedtschen Haus zur Marktstraße. Pferdekutschen und Bimmelbahnen starten von hier regelmäßig ihre gemütlichen Fahrten zum Schloss. Das Gadenstedtsche Haus (links) auf dem Oberpfarrkirchhof zeigt sich von außen heute noch fast so, wie es 1582 von dem einstigen Schlosshauptmann Dietrich von Gadenstedt hergerichtet wurde. Über einem steinernen Unterbau erhebt sich ein Fachwerkaufsatz, den ein kostbarer, wenn auch mittlerweile etwas aus dem rechten Maß geratener Erker dominiert. Reich geziert von Palmetten, Fächerrosetten, Blendarkaden sowie anderen renaissancetypischen Schmuckelementen und Symbolen steht dieser Erker wie das ganze Haus für den Stolz und Reichtum seines Bauherrn ebenso wie für die Kunstfertigkeit der damaligen Handwerker.

View from 'Gadenstedtsches Haus' to Marktstraße. Horse drawn carriages and model trains regularly start out their leisurely excursions up to the Castle. Today, 'Gadenstedtsches Haus' (left) at the high Parish churchyard appears almost exactly as when erected in 1582 by the former Captain of the Castle, Dietrich von Gadenstedt. The half-timbered upper section with a stone substructure is dominated by a valuable, albeit now disproportionately sized bay turret. Lavishly decorated with palms and fan rosettes, false arcade fronts and other typical Renaissance decorative features and symbols, this bay and the entire house represents the pride and wealth of its owner and serves as a testament to the skill of the craftsmen of the day.

Mit etwas Glück kann man von diesen Bänken aus einer Chorprobe der Schülerinnen und Schüler des Landesgymnasiums für Musik lauschen. Die für den Rundfunkjugendchor Wernigerode bekannte Bildungsstätte hat Unterrichts- und Probenräume im gegenüberliegenden „Alten Lyceum“, einem Schulgebäude aus dem Jahre 1730.

Seite 65: In der Breiten Straße 4 empfängt das gemütliche Café Wien seit 1897 seine Besucher in einem Fachwerkgebäude aus dem ausgehenden 16. Jahrhundert. Zu den prominentesten Gästen des Hauses gehören Hermann Löns und Ernst Barlach.

With a little luck, you can sit on these benches and listen to the pupils of the regional music school during choir practice. This well-known training institute for the Wernigerode radio broadcast youth choir has classrooms and rehearsal rooms in the “Altes Lyceum” opposite – a school building dating from 1730.

Page 65: At Breite Straße 4, the cosy Café Wien has welcomed guests since 1897 in this late 16th-century timber-framed building. The most prominent guests here included Hermann Löns and Ernst Barlach.

15
83
CAFE WIEN
CAFE WIEN
Café Wien
Café Wien
Café Wien

Kaum ein Reisender ahnt, dass auf dem Niko, wie die Wernigeröder kurz und knapp den beschaulichen Platz unweit des Marktes nennen, bis ins letzte Drittel des 19. Jahrhunderts die große Stadtkirche St. Nikolai gestanden hat; in der Pflasterung lässt sich der Grundriss des abgetragenen Gotteshauses jedoch nachvollziehen. Sofort in den Fokus der Passanten rückt hingegen der von Bernd Göbel geschaffene und im Juni 2003 eingeweihte Brunnen. Ein bronzener Punk sitzt auf dem Rand als heiliger Nikolaus von Myra; vor ihm, scheinbar über eine granitene Kugel gewachsen, ein Lebensbaum mit verschiedenen Personen, die der Stadt verbunden waren.
Auf nördlicher Seite wird der Platz von dem nach dem Stadtbrand von 1847 neu errichteten Gebäude des Nikolaihospitals begrenzt.

Most tourists hardly suspect that the Niko – as the locals refer to the quiet square not far from the market – was the location of the town's St Nicholas church until the last third of the 19th century. The paving stones clearly show the well-worn ground plan of the church. Passers-by immediately notice the fountain created by Bernd Göbel inaugurated in June 2003. A bronze punk perches on the edge as St Nicholas of Myra; and in front of him, as though the figure had grown up over a granite sphere, there is a tree of life showing various people connected to the town. On the northern side, the new St Nicholas hospital building, erected after the town fire of 1847, encloses the square.

Das 1229 mit dem Stadtrecht privilegierte Wernigerode gliederte sich bereits im 13. Jahrhundert in eine Alt- und in eine Neustadt. Letztere bewohnten vor allem Handwerker und Ackerbürger. Sie besaßen ihre geistliche Heimstatt in der Johanniskirche (links). Deren wuchtiger romanischer Westturm verleiht ihr die unverkennbar mittelalterliche Silhouette. Das Bildnis Martin Luthers (rechts) am Taufstein von St. Johannis erinnert an die frühe Reformation von Stadt und Grafschaft Wernigerode im 16. Jahrhundert. Aus der Zeit um 1500 stammt die Holzplastik Johannes des Täufers (unten).

Wernigerode was granted a town charter in 1229 and the old and new parts were already present in the 13th century. Mainly craftsmen and farming citizens lived in the new part of town. The church of St John (left) was their spiritual home. Its mighty Romanesque west tower reveals the unmistakeable mediaeval silhouette. The effigy of Martin Luther (above) on the baptismal font of St John is a reminder that early on in the 16th century the Reformation took place here and in the county of Wernigerode. The wooden sculpture of St John the Baptist dates from about 1500 (right).

In das Jahr 1415 wird der beeindruckende vierflüglige und doppelt klappbare Schnitzaltar (rechts) der Johanniskirche datiert. Die Maria mit dem Kinde in seinem Zentrum zeigte sich den Gläubigen früher nur zu Festtagen (links). An der Rückseite des linken Altarinnenflügels ist Christi Geburt zu sehen (unten).

St John's church has an impressive carved altarpiece consisting of four panels and double folding (right) and dating from 1415. The Virgin Mary and infant at the centre was formerly only shown to churchgoers on Sundays and festivals (left). The birth of Christ is depicted on the reverse of the left-hand internal wing of the altarpiece (above).

Seite 73: Der aus Berlin stammende Kornhändler Heinrich Krummel schuf mit dem 1674 von ihm errichteten Fachwerkhaus in Wernigerode ein besonderes Baudenkmal. Die barocken Reliefs in den Brüstungsfeldern geben bis heute Rätsel auf.

Page 73: Heinrich Krummel, a corn trader from Berlin, created a half-timbered house in 1674, which is now regarded as a special architectural monument in Wernigerode. The Baroque relief on the balustrades continue to present puzzles until this day.

Farbgebung an der Fassade des Krummelschen Hauses vor und nach der letzten Restaurierung.
The colour of the façade of the Krummel building before and after the last restoration.

„Thvt Busse"
"Do Penance"

„Gott liebet die Stadt umb Gerechtigkeit"
"God bless the town and justice"

Männer am Baum
Men at the tree

Stadt am Gewässer
Town by the water

ZIMMERVERMIT
Kosmetik-u.med.
Fußpflegestud
CAFE & BISTRO

Asienallegorie
Asian allegory

Frau mit Harnisch und Erdkugel
Lady with suit of armour and globe

„Ich richte undt nehme keine Geschencke von ungerechten"
"I judge and take no gifts from the unjust"

„Des Menschen Sterbligkeit"
"The mortality of man"

Bei der Bezeichnung der Erdteil-Allegorien „Africa" (links) und „America" (rechts) ist dem Schnitzer vermutlich eine Verwechslung unterlaufen.

When labelling allegories for the continents of "Africa" (left) and "America" (right), the craftsman probably made an error.

Die alten Fachwerkfassaden der Stadt warten, wie hier in der Breiten Straße, oft mit beachtenswerten Details auf: Eine Kartusche am Haus Nummer 44 (oben) erinnert an die Überwindung des großen Feuers von 1751.
Fächerpalmetten, Rollen sowie Schiffskehlen, renaissancetypische Schmuckelemente aus dem 16. Jahrhundert, schmücken das Obergeschoss der Nummer 62 (unten).

The town's old half-timbered façades are often decorated with remarkable details – as here, on Breite Straße: a cartouche scroll above number 44 (above) is a reminder of the battle against the great fire of 1751.
Fan palms, scrolls and ships coving – typical Renaissance decorative features dating from the 16th century – adorn the upper floor of number 62.

Im Lustgarten

Am Vorwerk

Der nordöstlich des Schlossberges gelegene Lustgarten wurde für das Landesprojekt „Gartenträume“ ausgewählt. Nach fachkundigen und aufwendigen Rekonstruktionsarbeiten in den Jahren 1992 und 2004/05 lädt er heute gleichermaßen zum Spazieren auf historischen Wegen und zum Toben auf dem Abenteuerspielplatz ein.

The pleasure garden situated north-east of the Castle was selected for the "GardenTräume" ("Garden Dreams") regional project. Following skilled and time-consuming reconstruction in 1992 and 2004/05, the garden is now a place to enjoy walks along historic routes or to have fun at the adventure play park.

Als Renaissancegarten im 16. Jahrhundert angelegt, erlebte der Park unter der Regie des Grafen Christian Ernst zu Stolberg-Wernigerode im 18. Jahrhundert eine großzügige barocke Umgestaltung. Die Orangerie und das restaurierte Löwentor sind steinerne Zeugen jener Epoche. Englischer Landschaftspark ist der Lustgarten seit dem frühen 19. Jahrhundert.
Die moderne Kunst unserer Tage ergänzt sein Ambiente stimmungsvoll: „Dem Leben gewidmet" von Achim Kühn vor der Orangerie (Seite 80) und „Touchstone" von Dietmar Bönisch (unten).

Cultivated as a 16th-century Renaissance garden, the park underwent generous Baroque redesign in the 18th century under the directorship of Count Christian Ernst zu Stolberg-Wernigerode. The orangery and restored lion gate are stone monuments dating from this period. The pleasure garden has been an English landscape garden since the early 19th century. Contemporary modern art adds to the appealing ambiance: "Dem Leben gewidmet" ("Dedication to Life") by Achim Kühn in front of the orangery (page 80), and "Touchstone" by Dietmar Bönisch (right).

Wer die nach dem Stadtbrand von 1751 neu errichtete Liebfrauenkirche (links) im Burgstraßenviertel betritt, findet sich in einem beinahe vollständig erhaltenen spätbarock-protestantischen Gotteshaus wieder. Das Gros der hölzernen Inneneinrichtung fertigte damals der Wernigeröder Hoftischler Johann Michael Möser. Zur Ausstattung gehört die sogenannte Fürstenloge mit einem lebensgroßen Kruzifix (rechts) direkt gegenüber dem Kanzelaltar (unten).

Anyone entering the newly renovated Church of Our Lady in the Burgstraße district (page 82) following the 1751 town fire arrives in an almost totally late Baroque Protestant church. Most of the wooden interiors date from this period and were produced by Johann Michael Möser, a local court cabinetmaker. They include the so-called prince's box with life-size crucifix (above) directly opposite the pulpit altar (left).

Östlicher Abschnitt der Breiten Straße. Der geschnitzte Koch am Eckgebäude zur Ringstraße steht für die gastliche Tradition des Hauses, in dem sich zum Beispiel zu DDR-Zeiten das Lokal „Zur Bunten Stadt“ befand.

The eastern section of Breite Straße. The carved chef on the corner building to Ringstraße stands for the tradition of hospitality where, for instance, in the days of the GDR, the “Zur Bunten Stadt” pub was located.

DER BÜCHERFREUND
Bücher

Das Handwerk besitzt in Wernigerode eine lange Geschichte. Vom letzten Drittel des 17. Jahrhunderts bis in das Jahr 1975 kamen beispielsweise in der Krellschen Schmiede Hammer und Amboss nicht zur Ruhe. Der Pferdekopf an der Hausfassade warb für eine Sattlerei, die auf dem gleichen Grundstück neben einer Stellmacherei ihre Dienste anbot.
Anno 2008 übernahm ein tatkräftiger Schmiedemeister die historische Werkstätte in der Breiten Straße 95. Er bringt seither regelmäßig das Feuer in der alten Esse zum Lodern.

In Wernigerode, handcrafted woodwork has a long tradition. From the last third of the 17th century until 1975, for instance, both hammer and anvil were scarcely out of use at the Krell Smithy. The horse's head on the building façade drew in trade for the saddlery on the same premises, adjacent to a wheelwright.
In 2008, a Master Blacksmith took over the historic workshop at Breite Straße 95 and is regularly at work in the old forge.

M·MICHEL KREL
ANNO
95
MARIA WERENPENIS
1678

Seite 88: Bis ins 14. Jahrhundert zurück reicht die Historie der St. Georgskapelle in der Ilsenburger Straße. Ursprünglich Teil eines von den Wernigeröder Grafen gestifteten Hospitals vor den Toren der Stadt, diente sie später als Wegekapelle. Ihre markante Fachwerkvorhalle besitzt sie seit 1635.

Familienfreundlich und jugendlich frisch gibt sich der 1907 eingemeindete Ortsteil Hasserode. Hier haben sich die Hochschule Harz mit der in einen kleinen Park integrierten Rektoratsvilla (rechts) und der Hasseröder Ferienpark (unten) etabliert.

Page 88: The history of St George's Chapel on Ilsenburger Straße dates back to the 14th century. Originally part of a hospital donated by the Count of Wernigerode and situated outside the town's gates, it later served as a wayside chapel. Its distinctive half-timbered entrance lobby dates from 1635.

The district of Hasserode incorporated into the town in 1907 is family-friendly and has a fresh, young look. This is the site of the Harz University of Applied Sciences with the small park and Rector's office (right) and Hasserode leisure and holiday park (below).

Volksbank
CAFE WIEN

„Harzblicke erleben", so lautete das Motto der 2006 in Wernigerode veranstalteten Landesgartenschau. 17 Hektar und damit ein Gutteil dieses im Norden der Stadt gelegenen Areals bilden heute den nicht nur von Gartenfreunden hoch geschätzten Bürgerpark. Seepromenade (oben) und Roter Baum haben wie die 78 Themengärten und das Zauberwäldchen dazu beigetragen, dass das Ensemble im Jahre 2008 zum drittschönsten Park Deutschlands gekürt wurde.
Neueste Attraktion im Bürgerpark ist der im Mai 2009 eröffnete „Kleine Harz" (links). Auf einer Fläche von 1,5 Hektar können hier solch bekannte Attraktionen wie die Kaiserpfalz Goslar, die Burg Falkenstein, das Brockenplateau und natürlich das Wernigeröder Rathaus im Miniaturformat 1:25 bestaunt werden.

"Harzblicke erleben" ("Views of the Harz Mountains") was the slogan for the 2006 Wernigerode Regional Garden Show. Today, the 17-hectare park and most of the town's northern part is not only a popular public park for the locals and garden lovers. The lake promenade (above) and Red Tree helped ensure that, along with the 78 themed gardens and magical miniature forest, in 2008, the complex was announced the third most beautiful park in Germany.
The latest attraction in the citizens' park is "Miniature Harz" which opened in May 2009 (left). Over 1.5 hectares, visitors can enjoy such well-known attractions as the Goslar Kaiserpfalz (Imperial Palace), Falkenstein Castle, the Brocken plateau and, of course, the miniature 1:25 version of Wernigerode Town Hall.

Im ganzjährig geöffneten Wildpark im Christianental leben über 40 verschiedene, meist heimische Wild- und Haustierarten, unter ihnen Luchs, Uhu und Damhirsch. Benannt nach dem Grafen Christian Ernst zu Stolberg-Wernigerode, gehörte dieses reizvolle Nebental des Nöschenröder Mühlentals mit seiner Gaststätte im Tiroler Stil (unten) einst zum fürstlichen Tiergarten.

In Christianental valley Game Park, open all year round, there are over 40 different and mostly native species of game and domestic animal species, including lynx, owl and fallow deer. Named after Count Christian Ernst zu Stolberg-Wernigerode, this charming subsidiary valley of the Nöschenröder Mühlental and its Tyrolean-style bar (below) was once a zoo on the count's estate.

Sikawild
Luchs

Das winterliche Hasserode.

Winter-time in Hasserode.

Sonnenuntergang am Waldgasthaus „Armeleuteberg“.

Sunset at the forest guesthouse, “Armeleuteberg”.

Der Wernigeröder Bürger Edmund Lührmann stiftete den Kaiserturm auf dem 478 Meter hohen Armeleuteberg. Zum Sedantag 1902 feierlich eingeweiht, gewährt er von seiner Plattform einen phantastischen Rundblick auf Stadt und Harz. Damals wie heute gilt übrigens, „daß der Turm offen steht und daß der Zutritt ohne Entree jedem freisteht."

Wernigerode citizen, Edmund Lührmann, donated the imperial tower on the 478-metre summit of Armeleuteberg. Inaugurated in 1902 on Sedan commemoration day, the tower's platform offers a fabulous panoramic view of the town and Harz Mountains. Then, as now, however, "the tower is open to everyone and the public is granted free access".

Gustav

Viele Häuser in Nöschenrode unterscheiden sich, abgesehen von ihrer landschaftlichen Lage, kaum von denen in der Altstadt. Dabei befand sich der heutige Ortsteil noch bis zum weitgehenden Abbruch der Wernigeröder Stadtbefestigung außerhalb des sicheren Mauerrings. Erst 1929 und nach langem Widerstand ihrer Bewohner wurde die Vorstadt nach Wernigerode eingemeindet.

Historische Häuserzeile in der Promenade unmittelbar am Zillierbach (links) und schmuckvolle Details am Gebäude der Nöschenröder Straße 59 (unten).

With the exception of their position, many houses in Nöschenrode are scarcely any different from those in the Old Town. Today, this part of the town district was beyond the perimeter of the secure inner ring until the widespread demolition of Wernigerode town's former fortification. Not until 1929 and only after long opposition from their inhabitants were the suburbs integrated into Wernigerode town.

The historic row of houses on the promenade directly at Zillierbach (left) and decorative details on the building at Nöschenröder Straße 59 (above).

Am Eingang des Nöschenröder Friedhofs erhebt sich die Theobaldikapelle (rechts) aus der zweiten Hälfte des 13. Jahrhunderts. Etwa 150 Jahre später erhielt sie ihre Kreuzform. Die Gelder für den Ausbau hatte Heinrich, der letzte Graf von Wernigerode, gestiftet. Vieles spricht dafür, dass er auf diese Weise die Missetaten seines 1386 wegen Landfriedensbruchs hingerichteten Bruders Dietrich sühnen wollte.

Das Mausoleum der Grafen zu Stolberg-Wernigerode (links) entstand aus Haustein in neoromanischen Formen Mitte des 19. Jahrhunderts. Schräg gegenüber kann man historische Grabplatten entdecken, darunter die des Fürsten Otto zu Stolberg-Wernigerode (unten).

Theobaldi Chapel (page 101) is located at the entrance to Nöschenrode cemetery and dates from the second half of the 13th century. Its cross shape originated from about 150 years later. Heinrich, the last Count of Wernigerode, donated the funds for the extension. It is likely that he hoped to make amends for the misdeeds of his brother, Dietrich, who was executed for a public breach of the peace.

The mausoleum of the Counts zu Stolberg-Wernigerode (above) was created from cut stone in neo-Romanesque forms in the mid-19th century. Diagonally opposite, the historic headstones can be discovered, including that of Prince Otto zu Stolberg-Wernigerode (right).

Ruhestätte Familie
Karnapke

Das Schiff der Theobaldikapelle (Seite 102) ist geprägt von farbenfrohen barocken Ausmalungen aus dem späten 17. Jahrhundert. Szenen des Alten und Neuen Testaments schmücken die Brüstungen der Emporen.
Die originale Bemalung hat sich auch in der Holztonne erhalten. Hier ist in kraftvoll-naivem Stil ein blauer Himmel mit einigen prallen Wölkchen gespannt, aus dem Engel auf den Betrachter herabschauen (links).
Die Predella des Altars ist mit fünf Reliquienbüsten besetzt. Eine von Ihnen zeigt den Namenspatron Theobald (unten).

The nave of Theobaldi Chapel (left) is influenced by brightly coloured Baroque paintings dating from the late 17th century. Old and New Testament scenes adorn the balustrades on the galleries.
The original painting on the wooden barrel-vaulting was also preserved. Here, in bold and naive style, a blue sky is filled with a few intense clouds and angels looking down on the viewer (above).
The altarpiece's predella has five busts with relics, one of which displays Theobald, the patron saint (right).

Einst wehrhafte Grafenburg, später fürstliche Residenz, seit 1949 viel besuchtes Museum – Schloss Wernigerode gilt als eines der schönsten Bergschlösser Deutschlands. Nach seinem Umbau 1862 bis 1885 zählte das Haus 59 Repräsentations- und Wohnräume, 31 Zimmer für Angestellte und Bedienstete, 38 Vorrats- und Abstellkammern, 35 Flure und Vorräume sowie 22 größere Korridore. Noch bis in das Jahr 1929 bewohnte die fürstliche Familie derer zu Stolberg-Wernigerode ihren angestammten Sitz. An die als uneinnehmbar geltende Feste des Spätmittelalters erinnern noch heute unter anderem einige Ringmauerzüge sowie der 1417 erstmals schriftlich erwähnte Hausmanns- oder Schusterturm (vorn links).

Once the defensive Grafenburg, later a princely residence, since 1949 a much-visited museum – Castle Wernigerode is regarded as one of the most beautiful mountain castles in Germany. After its renovation from 1862 to 1885, the building included 59 representational and living rooms, 31 rooms for employees and public servants, 38 pantries and storehouses, 35 halls and reception rooms as well as 22 larger corridors. Until 1929, the zu Stolberg-Wernigerode family still lived in their residence. Several curtain wall tracts and the shoemaker's tower, first mentioned in 1417 (front left), are still reminiscent today of the impregnable ramparts of the late-mediaeval period.

Als museale Einrichtung hat sich das Schloss besonders der Kunst- und Kulturgeschichte des 19. Jahrhunderts verschrieben. In der ganzjährig geöffneten Dauerausstellung sind beispielsweise die 2009 teils mit Originalmöbeln eingerichtete „Rote Henrichskammer“ (oben) und der ganz in historistischer Manier ausgestaltete Festsaal (rechts) zu besichtigen. An den Saalwänden setzte der bekannte Münchner Historienmaler Konrad Beckmann wichtige Ereignisse aus der Geschichte des hochadeligen Hauses Stolberg-Wernigerode wirkungsvoll in Szene.

The museum located in the Castle is dedicated, above all, to art and cultural history of the 19th century. In the year-round permanent exhibition, for example, "Rote Henrichskammer" ("Red Henrich Chamber", above) is partly furnished with original pieces and the historicist banqueting hall (right) is open to the public. On the walls of the hall, the well-known Munich history painter, Konrad Beckmann, impressively captured the major events in the history of the Stolberg-Wernigerode dynasty.

Auf und ab geht es im Schloss in insgesamt vier Treppentürmen, auf zehn Wendeltreppen und 85 weiteren Treppen. Der Wendelstieg im Fahnenturm bildet heute den Auftakt für jeden Museumsbesuch. Über seine 51 Stufen gelangt man in den Schlossinnenhof.

Up and down in the Castle – over a total of four staircase turrets and ten spiral staircases with 85 additional stairways. The spiral staircase in the flag tower is nowadays a prelude to every museum visit. Its 51 steps lead up to the castle interior.

Details in der zu Ostern 1880 neu geweihten Schlosskirche St. Pantaleon und St. Anna: spätmittelalterliche Madonnenplastik (rechts) und Gewölbeschlussstein mit dem Wappen des Hauses Stolberg-Wernigerode (unten).

Details in the Castle church St Pantaleon and St Anna, newly consecrated at Easter 1880 – late-mediaeval sculptures of the Holy Virgin (right) and the vaulting boss with the coat-of-arms of the house of Stolberg-Wernigerode (above).

Seit 1999 trägt Schloss Wernigerode samt der dazugehörigen Park- und Gartenanlagen das Prädikat „national wertvolles Kulturdenkmal". Viele der Ausstellungsräume vermitteln einen authentischen Eindruck von der Wohnkultur des deutschen Hochadels im 19. Jahrhundert. Als Besuchermagneten erweisen sich immer wieder das mit dem Originalinterieur ausgestattete Schreibzimmer des Grafen Otto zu Stolberg-Wernigerode (unten) und die jahrhundertealten Harnische im barocken Sommerbau (rechts).

Seite 111: Aussicht vom Fahnenturm.

Since 1999, Castle Wernigerode and the adjoining park and gardens have been declared a "national cultural monument". Many of the exhibition rooms offer an authentic impression of the lifestyle of Germany's high nobility during the 19th century. Top visitor attractions include Count Otto zu Stolberg-Wernigerode's study with its original interior (left) and the century-old suit of armour in the Baroque summer building (above).

Page 111: View from the flag tower.

Der Schlossinnenhof bietet für Konzert- und Opernaufführungen eine märchenhafte Kulisse. Ein Höhepunkt sind hier die alljährlich stattfindenden Wernigeröder Schlossfestspiele. Im Sommer 2009 begeisterten Gastvokalisten und die Musiker des Philharmonischen Kammerorchesters Wernigerode mit der Mozart-Oper „Cosi fan tutte".

Die sorgsam restaurierte und seit Sommer 2006 wieder zugängliche Weinbergterrasse auf Schloss Wernigerode (links) zählt zu den „Gartenträumen". Dieses touristische Landesprojekt verbindet 40 historische Park- und Gartenanlagen Sachsen-Anhalts miteinander.

The Castle's inner courtyard is a prefect setting for concert and opera performances and a fairytale backdrop. A highlight here is the annual Wernigerode Castle Festival Season. During the summer of 2009, guest vocalists and musicians from Wernigerode Philharmonic Chamber Orchestra gave a delightful performance of Mozart's "Cosi fan tutte".

The vineyard terrace at Wernigerode Castle (left), which was carefully restored and has been accessible again since the summer of 2006, is part of "Garden Dreams". This regional tourist project connects 40 historic park and garden sites in Saxony-Anhalt.

Seit 1899 dampft die Harzquer- und Brockenbahn von Wernigerode aus über den Harz. Ihre Züge beförderten im Jahre 2009 gemeinsam mit der Selketalbahn insgesamt 1 160 000 Fahrgäste und davon allein etwa 726 000 unmittelbar auf Norddeutschlands höchsten Berg. Das Streckennetz dieser historischen Eisenbahn umfasst 140 Kilometer samt 400 Brücken und Durchlässen. Der bekannteste ihrer 44 Bahnhöfe und Haltepunkte befindet sich direkt auf dem Brocken in einer Höhe von 1 125 m üNN.
Zum Fahrzeugbestand der Harzer Schmalspurbahnen gehören unter anderem 25 historische Dampflokomotiven, von denen die meisten zwischen 1954 und 1956 gebaut wurden. Ganz weit oben in der Gunst der Eisenbahnfreunde rangieren die um 1900 gefertigten Malletlokomotiven (oben).

Seite 116/117: Ob zu Fuß, per Fahrrad, mit dem Pferdefuhrwerk oder der Schmalspurbahn, auf das Plateau des 1 141 Meter hohen Brocken ist es von Wernigerode aus fast nur ein Katzensprung.

Since 1899, the Trans-Harz and Brocken railway steams ahead from Wernigerode across the Harz Mountains. In 2009, the trains and those of the Selketal railway carried a total of 1,160,000 visitors and 726,000 alone travelled to north Germany's highest peak. This historic transport network includes of 140 km with 400 bridges and passes. The best-known of the 44 stations and stops is directly on the Brocken, 1,125 m above sea level.
The engines of the Harz Narrow Gauge railway include, among others, 25 historic steam locomotives, most of which were built between 1954 and 1956. The Mallet locomotives dating from about 1900 (above) are held in high esteem by railway enthusiasts.

Page 116/117: Whether on foot, by bicycle, by horse-drawn carriage or narrow gauge railway, the plateau of the 1,141-metre Brocken is a stone's throw from Wernigerode.

99 7241-5

Von der vereisten Teufelskanzel auf dem Brocken geht der Blick über den Königsberg zum 971 Meter hohen Wurmberg. Speziell der schauerlichen Mär von der alljährlichen Hexenfahrt verdankt der sagenumwobene Blocksberg seit eh und je Respekt und Popularität. Im Aufklärungszeitalter bestiegen ihn unter anderem Otto von Guericke und Zar Peter I.; Goethe und Heine folgten und ließen sich wie viele andere Künstler von ihren ganz persönlichen Gipfelerlebnissen inspirieren. Die touristische Erschließung des Berges begann bereits im 18. Jahrhundert. So ließ Graf Christian Ernst zu Stolberg-Wernigerode 1736 unmittelbar auf dem Plateau ein steinernes Schutzhaus errichten. Jenes „Wolkenhäuschen" konnte seinen angestammten Platz bis in die Gegenwart standhaft behaupten.

From the icy Devil's Turret on the Brocken, there is a view across Königsberg to the 971-metre high Wurmberg. In particular, the gruesome legend of the annual witches' flight means that Blocksberg, which is surrounded by myths and fairytales, has earned respect and popularity. During the Enlightenment, for example, Otto von Guericke and Tsar Peter I. climbed the Brocken – Goethe and Heine followed and, as other artists before and after, were inspired by their intensely personal experiences at the summit. Tourist access to the peak had already begun in the 18th century. For instance, Count Christian Ernst zu Stolberg-Wernigerode founded a stone shelter on the plateau. This "cloud hut" has remained intact in the same place until the present day.

Der Hohnekamm südöstlich des Brockenmassivs begeistert mit seiner urwüchsigen Vegetation und zahlreichen Granitklippen. Ab Oktober 1990 gehörten Hohnekamm und Brocken zu dem in Sachsen-Anhalt gelegenen Nationalpark Hochharz. Dieser fusionierte 2006 mit dem niedersächsischen Nationalpark Harz.

Seite 121: Die Alte Schmiede (oben) erinnert an die Ursprünge des Forst- und Hüttenortes Schierke, der sich ab dem Ausgang des 19. Jahrhunderts zu einem der beliebtesten Sommer- wie Winterurlaubsplätze des Harzes entwickelte. Das seinerzeit mondäne „St. Moritz des Nordens" wurde 2009 samt Brocken nach Wernigerode eingemeindet.
Direkt oberhalb des Kurparks befindet sich das Schierker Rathaus (unten).

The Hohnekamm, south-east of the Brocken summit, is inspiring with its earthy vegetation and numerous granite cliffs. Since October 1990, Hohnekamm and Brocken belonged to the Hochharz National Park situated in Saxony-Anhalt. In 2006, this was merged with Lower Saxony's Harz National Park.

Page 121: The Old Forge (above) is reminiscent of the original forestry and wooden-hut hamlet of Schierke, which evolved in the late 19th century to one of the most popular summer- and winter holiday locations in the Harz. In 2009, the once sophisticated "St Moritz of the North" was integrated into Wernigerode along with the Brocken peak.
Schierke Town Hall is located directly above the spa park (below).

Alte Schmiede
Hotel „Bodeblick"
Barenberg
Zahnarzt
Haus Forellengrund
Kantorstübchen
Friseur Heidenreich
Für Sie und Ihn
Altbau-Apartments
Hotel König
China-Restaurant
Pension Schmidt

Schon seit 1993 gehören die unmittelbar am Harzrand bzw. im Harzvorland gelegenen Dörfer Benzingerode, Minsleben und Silstedt zu Wernigerode. Während die Silstedter bereits 1995 die 1000. Wiederkehr der ersten urkundlichen Nennung ihres Ortes feierten, beging die Minslebener Bevölkerung dieses Fest im Jahre 2000. Die schriftlich überlieferte Geschichte Benzingerodes reicht bis in das frühe 13. Jahrhundert zurück. Eine Attraktion des Ortes ist der unlängst sanierte und wieder zu besichtigende mittelalterliche Wartturm auf dem Austberg (links).

Jüngstes Mitglied der Wernigeröder Kommune ist seit dem 1. Januar 2010 die Vorharzgemeinde Reddeber, die stolz darauf verweisen kann, in einer ottonischen Urkunde aus dem Jahre 936 als „Rudiburgi" benannt worden zu sein. Am Ortsausgang nach Minsleben wird mit einem Denkmal den Gefallenen beider Weltkriege gedacht (unten).

Since 1993, the villages of Benzingerode, Minsleben and Silstedt situated on the immediate periphery of the Harz or in the outlying area have belonged to Wernigerode.
While the people of Silstedt already celebrated the 1000th anniversary of the first recorded mention of their town, the Minsleben population celebrated this festival in 2000. Benzingerode's written history dates back to the early 13th century. An attraction of this location is the recently renovated mediaeval watch tower on Austberg which can be visited again (above).

Since 1 January 2010, the most recent member of Wernigerode municipality is the outlying community of Reddeber, which can proudly record its inclusion as the "Rudiburgi" in a charter by Otto dating from the year 936. On the way out of the village, en route for Minsleben, a monument commemorates the fallen of both world wars (right).

Pünktlich zur 1000-Jahrfeier wurde in Silstedt der Museumshof „Ernst Koch" eröffnet (unten). Die mit Originalinventar ausgestatteten Räume wie Stube, Küche und Schlafzimmer lassen nebst zahlreicher landwirtschaftlicher Geräte auf dem Hof den dörflichen Alltag vergangener Zeiten lebendig werden.

Right on time for the 1000th anniversary, the "Ernst Koch" museum courtyard was opened in Silstedt (below). The rooms furnished with original pieces such as lounge, kitchen and bedroom and numerous agricultural pieces of equipment revitalise the bygone days of village life in this courtyard.

Seite 124: Die weithin sichtbare, in Teilen noch romanische St. Margarethenkirche von Minsleben dankt ihre Ersterwähnung einem 1327 aufgesetzten Dokument.

Page 124: The visible, and in parts the still Romanesque St Margarethen Church of the Parish of Minsleben owes its first mention to a document recorded in 1327.

Titelbild: Rathaus Wernigerode
Seite 2/3: Blick vom Turm der Liebfrauenkirche zum Schlossberg
Rückseite: Fachwerkdetails am Neustädter Rathaus

Bibliografische Information Der Deutschen Bibliothek
Die Deutsche Bibliothek verzeichnet diese Publikation in der Deutschen Nationalbibliografie; detaillierte bibliografische Daten sind im Internet über http://dnb.ddb.de abrufbar.

Bildnachweis:
Seite 89 unten Hasseröder Ferienpark; Seite 113 Matthias Bein; Seite 118 bis 120 Dr. Uwe Lagatz; Seite 25 unten, 26, 27, 106 bis 112 © Schloß Wernigerode® GmbH, Aufnahmen Thorsten Schmidt

Lektorat: Marion Schmidt
Übersetzung/Translation: ConText Communication – Übersetzer | Texter | Lektoren, Mainz

Die Winde 45; D - 38855 Wernigerode
Tel.: (0 39 43) 2 32 46 • Fax: (0 39 43) 4 50 10 • info@schmidt-buch-verlag.de

1. Auflage 2010, 1. - 6. Tsd.
Satz, Gestaltung, Bildbearbeitung, Kartografie: Schmidt-Buch-Verlag, Wernigerode
Druck und Weiterverarbeitung: Grafisches Centrum Cuno GmbH & Co. KG, Calbe

Internet: www.schmidt-buch-verlag.de

Flexcover ISBN 978-3-936185-61-4
Hardcover ISBN 978-3-936185-62-1

1 Rathaus *town hall*
2 „Gothisches Haus“ *„gothic house“*
3 „Weißer Hirsch“ *„white deer“*
4 Marktbrunnen *market fountain*
5 Café Wien *Café Vienna*
6 Nikolaiplatz mit Brunnen *Square of St. Nicholas and fountain*
7 Brunnenhof
8 Krummelsches Haus
9 Krellsche Schmiede *Krell smithy*
10 Angerhof
11 ehem. Orangerie *former orangery*
12 Halbschalentürme in der Stadtmauer *half-open towers in the town wall*
13 Schloß Wernigerode® *Wernigerode castle*
14 Mausoleum und Gräber der Grafen zu Stolberg-Wernigerode *Mausoleum and headstones of the Counts zu Stolberg-Wernigerode*
15 Theobaldikapelle *Theobaldi Chapel*
16 zum Tierpark Christianental *to the Game Park Christian valley*
17 schmuckvolle Details am Haus Nr. 59 *decorative details on house No. 59*
18 zur Harburg *to Harburg*
19 zum Armeleuteberg/Kaiserturm *to the Armeleuteberg/imperial tower*
20 Liebfrauenkirche *Church of Our Lady*
21 Kleinstes Haus *town's smallest house*
22 Skulpturen in der Marktstraße *sculptures in market street*
23 Schiefes Haus *Crooked House*
24 St. Sylvestrikirche *St Sylvestri Church*
25 Harzmuseum mit Harzbücherei *Harz Museum and regional library*
26 Westerntorturm *Westerntor Tower*
27 St. Georgskapelle *St George's Chapel*
28 St. Johanniskirche *Church of St John*

Citybus line coach
Bahnen zum Schloss „trains“ to the castle
Wohnmobilstellplatz Camper parking lot
Gartenträume-Projekt garden dreams project
Postagentur post office
Tankstelle filling station
Einbahnstraße one-way street
Parkplatz parking lot
Museum museum
Kirche church
Schloss castle
Burgbreite
Voßberg
287
Kleingärten
Kastanienwäldchen
Platz des Friedens
GWW
Altenheim
Schule
Sporthalle
Sportplatz
Karl-Marx-Straße
Kopernikusstr.
Halberstädter Straße
„Anger/Schloss“
Lustgarten
Spielplatz
Planetarium
Am Lustgarten
ehem. Marstall
Im Rosenwinkel
Augustenallee
Silbertanne
Konstantinstein
Agnesberg
395
ehemaliger fürstlicher Tiergarten
Altar der Wahrheit
Schloss
Schlosskirche
Nationalparkverwaltung
Sonderschule
Robert-Koch-Institut
Schmatzfelder Str.
DB Bhf
Bus Bhf
HSB-Endpunkt
Arbeitsagentur
Amtsgericht
Feuerwehr
Altstadtkreisel
Bahnhofstr.
Vor der Mauer
244
Gymnasium
Kultursaal
Altstadt-Passagen
Polizei
Breite Straße
Sebastian-Bach-Straße
IHK
Suchtberatung
Ringerhalle
Nöschenröder Straße
Theobaldi-friedhof
Mühlental
Nöschenrode
Seigerhüttenteich
Kleingärten
Im Stadtfelde
Feldstraße
Kohlgartenstr.
Großer Christianentalweg
Kleiner Christianentalweg
Totenweg
Pulvergarten
Harburgstraße
Gartenstraße